THE DOUBLE V CAMPAIGN

ALSO BY MICHAEL L. COOPER

HELL FIGHTERS
African American Soldiers in World War I

BOUND FOR THE PROMISED LAND
The Great Black Migration

FROM SLAVE TO CIVIL WAR HERO
The Life and Times of Robert Smalls

PLAYING AMERICA'S GAME
The Story of Negro League Baseball

THE DOUBLE V CAMPAIGN

African Americans and World War II

MICHAEL L. COOPER

LODESTAR BOOKS
Dutton   New York

to Ruth, Paul, and David

Library of Congress Cataloging-in-Publication Data

Cooper, Michael L., 1950–
   The double V campaign: African Americans and World War II / Michael L.
Cooper.—1st ed.
      p.   cm.
   Includes bibliographical references and index.
   Summary: Recounts how African Americans fought two wars during World
War II, one against enemy dictators abroad and the other against racial
discrimination at home.
   ISBN 0-525-67562-0 (alk. paper)
   1. World War, 1939–1945—Participation, Afro-American—Juvenile
literature.   2. United States—Armed Forces—Afro-Americans—Juvenile
literature.   3. Afro-Americans—Segregation—Juvenile literature.
4. Racism—United States—Juvenile literature.   5. United States—Race
relations—Juvenile literature. [1. World War, 1939–1945—Participation,
Afro-American.   2. United States—Armed Forces—Afro-Americans.
3. Afro-Americans—Segregation.   4. Racism.   5. United States—Race
relations.]
I. Title.
D810.N4C66   1998
940.54′03—dc21   97-28229   CIP   AC

Published in the United States by Lodestar Books,
an affiliate of Dutton Children's Books,
a member of Penguin Putnam Inc.,
375 Hudson Street, New York, New York 10014

Published simultaneously in Canada
by McClelland & Stewart, Toronto

Editor: Virginia Buckley   Designer: Dick Granald

Printed in Hong Kong   First Edition
2 4 6 8 10 9 7 5 3 1

Contents

World War II in the Pacific

Mongolia

Manchuria

Beijing

China

Korea

Tibet

Tokyo

India

Japan

Shanghai

Kunming

Burma Road

Taiwan

Lashio

Burma

Hong Kong

Rangoon

Bataan
Dec. 1941–
April 1942

Luzon

Manila

Guam

Thailand

Indochina

Philippines

Indian
Ocean

Mindanao

Carolin

South
China
Sea

Equator

Malaya

Singapore

Equator

New Guinea

Sumatra

Borneo

Netherlands   Indies

Papua

Java Sea
Feb. 1942

Port Moresby

| 0 | 500 | 1,000 Miles |

| 0 | 1,000 Kilometers |

Darwin

Australia

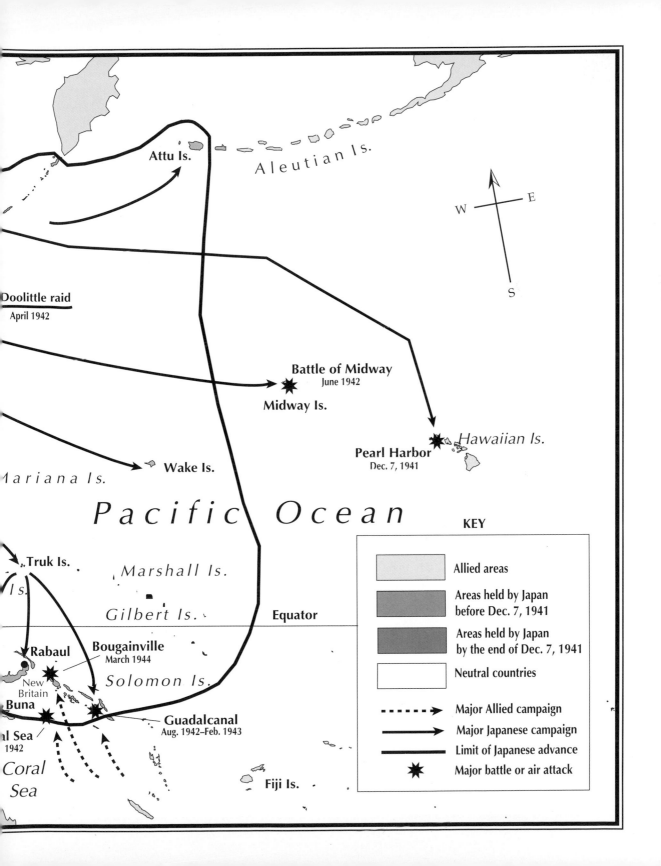

Attu Is.

Aleutian Is.

W — E

S

Doolittle raid
April 1942

Battle of Midway
June 1942

Midway Is.

Pearl Harbor
Dec. 7, 1941

Hawaiian Is.

Wake Is.

Mariana Is.

Pacific Ocean

KEY

Truk Is.

Marshall Is.

Is.

Gilbert Is.

Equator

Rabaul

Bougainville
March 1944

Solomon Is.

New
Britain

Buna

Guadalcanal
Aug. 1942–Feb. 1943

al Sea

1942

Coral
Sea

Fiji Is.

	Allied areas
	Areas held by Japan before Dec. 7, 1941
	Areas held by Japan by the end of Dec. 7, 1941
	Neutral countries
---▶	Major Allied campaign
▶	Major Japanese campaign
—	Limit of Japanese advance
✴	Major battle or air attack

World War II in Europe

Sea

Volga R.

Moscow

U. S. S. R.

✳ Kursk
July 1943

● Stalingrad

*Caspian
Sea*

●Yalta

Black Sea

Turkey

Iran

Syria
(Fr.)

Iraq

rus
.B.)   Lebanon

Palestine
(G.B.)   Transjordan
(G.B.)

Suez
Canal

Saudi
Arabia

n

Cairo ●

☐	Allied countries
■	Germany 1942–1945
▨	Other Axis countries and occupied areas
▨	Neutral countries
—▷	Major Allied campaign
- - - -	Limit of Allied advance
——	Limit of Axis advance
✳	Major battle

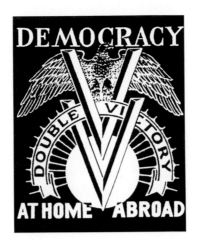

The Double Victory Campaign

When African Americans demanded to fight on the front lines in World War II, they were not being exceptionally brave. Blacks wanted to shoulder the responsibilities of citizenship in order to win their own long battle for equality in the United States. The war was a good opportunity to fight for civil rights.

The Pittsburgh *Courier* gave this two-sided fight a symbol by proclaiming the "Double V," or double victory, Campaign. The influential black-owned newspaper wanted its readers to wage two wars: one against enemy dictators abroad and the other against racial discrimination at home.

African Americans first wanted jobs—both in the military and in civilian life—that were being denied them because of their color. In the beginning, their demands were stubbornly resisted, but the growing war emergency weakened that resistance. America's political leaders were willing to break down the barriers of discrimination because the nation needed the support of all of its citizens to win the war.

Adolf Hitler, the German dictator, started World War II. Hitler wanted the Germans, who he said were a superior race of people, to rule the world. The dictator claimed other races, especially Jews and blacks, were inferior. His regime imprisoned and murdered six million Jewish men, women, and children. This horrible crime became known as the Holocaust.

In 1939, German soldiers overran the little nation of Poland. Next, Hitler's powerful army invaded Holland, Belgium, Luxembourg, and France. By 1941, Germany controlled all of western Europe except Great Britain, an island nation separated from the European Continent by the English Channel.

Across the Atlantic Ocean, Americans felt distant and safe from the European war, but the conflict quickly changed their lives. The United States sided with Great Britain. "We must become the great arsenal of democracy," declared President Franklin D. Roosevelt. America began shipping the embattled British millions of tons of food and weapons, which had a big impact on America's economy. The United States, like the world's other industrial countries, had been suffering for a decade under a financial crisis called the Great Depression. One-fourth of all adults were unemployed. World War II ended the Depression by putting millions of Americans back to work and by returning the nation to prosperity.

The Japanese, who were allies of the Germans, bombed Pearl Harbor in late 1941, forcing the United States into war. Millions of American men and women left their homes to serve in the armed forces. Over a million African Americans were among them, but the military's blatant discrimination blunted their enthusiasm.

Neither the navy, the marines, nor the air force wanted black recruits. Most African Americans served in the army, the largest branch of the armed services, but the army discriminated in training, living quarters, and duty assignments. This lack of respect caused bitter resentment. Fights and even gun battles between blacks and whites became common on army bases. Yet, the war crisis and the demands of black leaders quickly forced the armed forces to begin treating African Americans fairly.

By war's end, the changes in the military had been dramatic. Black Americans were serving in all branches of the armed forces. They performed every kind of job from tank driver to fighter pilot, and they served in all ranks, from private to general. African American soldiers were honored for heroism in battles against the Japanese in the Pacific and against the Germans in Europe.

The Double V Campaign was a fight to preserve and expand democracy and freedom both abroad and at home. It was waged by tens of thousands of black men and women. Some were prominent leaders, but most were ordinary citizens and soldiers who simply wanted the chance to use their skills and talents in ways that would best help the nation.

African Americans had been willing to serve and, if necessary, to die for their country, but in return they wanted equal responsibilities and equal opportunities. The Double V Campaign "is no fight merely to wear a uniform," explained one African American newspaper editor. "This is a struggle for status, a struggle to take democracy off a parchment and give it life."

1

Fighting for the Right To Fight

"Why should I shed my blood for Roosevelt's America," fumed an African American writer, "for the whole Jim Crow, Negro-hating South, for the low-paid, dirty jobs for which Negroes have to fight, for the few dollars of relief, and insults, discrimination, police brutality, and perpetual poverty to which Negroes are condemned even in the more liberal North?"

This writer was angry that African American soldiers would be dying for a country that had always treated them badly. Other black Americans expressed resentment too, but they also felt a patriotic duty to fight for their nation. These conflicting feelings were resolved by the Pittsburgh *Courier's* Double V Campaign which was embraced by many black publications, churches, and ordinary people.

The campaign was popular because blacks were still bitter over their treatment in World War I, only two decades earlier. White people had believed "colored" men were neither smart enough nor brave enough to be combat soldiers. Most of the four hundred thousand black soldiers in that first war with Germany were assigned jobs as laborers, doing little more than unloading ships or chopping wood. They returned home expecting their military service to be respected, but whites beat up and even murdered black veterans.

African Americans were also angry because they too had suffered extreme poverty during the Great Depression, but black men and women were not being hired for war-industry jobs. Factories displayed signs that read HELP WANTED—WHITE ONLY. A spokesman for the Standard Steel Company of Kansas City stated bluntly, "We've never hired a Negro worker and don't intend to start now."

Discrimination was a common part of daily life. Black people had to drink from separate water fountains and use separate public restrooms marked with signs that read COLORED ONLY. They were not allowed to sit beside white people in restaurants or on buses and trains. Three-fourths of African Americans lived in the South, and life for them was much worse there.

In Louisiana, Georgia, South Carolina, and other states of the old Confederacy, blacks were denied every basic American freedom. They could not vote or express their opinions freely. Southern blacks lived in constant fear. A white man could burn a black family's home or murder someone in their family for being "uppity" and not be arrested. Children attended segregated schools, which were so poor young people did not learn to adequately read or write. Adults were limited to working as servants or as field hands. These low-paying jobs kept them in poverty and in constant need of such basics as clothing, warm homes, and even food.

African Americans were weary and resentful of the prejudice they endured daily. They scoffed when the nation's leaders, appealing to traditional democratic ideals to encourage citizens to support the war, spoke as though all Americans were treated equally. President Roosevelt, in a famous speech early in 1941, emphasized the need to fight to protect "four essential human freedoms"—freedom of speech, freedom of religion, freedom from want, freedom from fear. African American leaders emphasized these same ideals—and the fact that no black American enjoyed these four freedoms—in their Double V Campaign.

"If we fail to fight to make the democratic process work in America while we fight to beat down Japan and Hitler," declared A. Philip Randolph, "we will be traitors to democracy and liberty and to the liberation of the Negro people."

Randolph, the president of the Brotherhood of Sleeping Car Porters, the nation's largest black union, had been a prominent civil rights leader for thirty years. He had a bold idea. "I suggest that ten thousand Negroes march on Washington, D.C.," Randolph declared, "with the slogan We Loyal Americans Demand the Right To Work and Fight for Our Country." He scheduled the march, the first big black demonstration ever planned for the nation's capital, for July 1, 1941.

Some African Americans objected to Randolph's plan. "Blacks could demand their full citizenship rights after Hitler and the Axis powers had been defeated. Everything must be sacrificed in winning this war," argued a chapter director of the National Association for the Advancement of Colored People (NAACP). Most other black leaders, such as Mary McLeod Bethune, a prominent educator and member of the Roosevelt administration, and Walter White, president of the NAACP, supported the march.

Randolph wanted President Roosevelt to order army generals and factory owners to end discrimination against African Americans. Blacks should have the same job opportunities white Americans enjoyed. The U.S. government always exercises more power over businesses and ordinary citizens in time of war, or threat of war, than in time of peace. The president of the United States could tell the nation's factories whom to hire.

"The Negroes' stake in national defense is big," Randolph said. "It consists of jobs, thousands of jobs. It may represent millions, yes, hundreds of millions of dollars in wages. It consists of new industrial opportunities and hope. This is worth fighting for."

Enthusiasm for the march grew as summer approached. Organizers held rallies in the black neighborhoods of Harlem, Chicago, and Cleveland. This support encouraged Randolph to expect ten times as many people than he first estimated. "When one hundred thousand Negroes march on Washington," he declared, "it will wake up Negro as well as white America."

The protest march, as Randolph had planned, worried Roosevelt. The president knew it was crucial for the nation to work together to win the war and that a huge

Black protesters urged people not to participate in the war effort.

demonstration might divide America. In mid-June, Roosevelt invited Walter White and Randolph to the White House to talk.

At their meeting, the president got directly to the point, "How many people will really march?"

"No less than one hundred thousand," White replied.

Roosevelt looked the NAACP leader directly in the eye for several seconds, trying to determine whether the number was an honest prediction or a bluff.

A. Philip Randolph and Eleanor Roosevelt in 1943

Finally, he asked, "What do you want me to do?"

"We would like," Randolph replied, "a presidential order that would abolish discrimination in the war industries and in the armed forces."

As a result of that meeting, Roosevelt issued Executive Order 8802, which established the Fair Employment Practices Commission. It outlawed job discrimination against all ethnic groups. "If this order is made workable and effective," declared the enthusiastic editors of the Pittsburgh *Courier*, "the thirteen million Negroes in the United

States can very well proclaim it to be an economic Emancipation Proclamation."

Opposition to the commission was immediate. "All the armies of the world," warned a white newspaperman in Louisville, Kentucky, "could not force upon the South the abandonment of racial segregation." Some Americans were in no mood to be fair, and discrimination would continue for years. But these concerns were abruptly pushed aside by the war.

On December 7, 1941, Japanese fighter planes attacked the U.S. Navy fleet at Pearl Harbor in Hawaii. It was "a date which will live in infamy," said President Roosevelt. On that horrible day in Hawaii, one of the first American heroes of World War II was a black man.

2

Pearl Harbor

Early Sunday morning, Dorie Miller and twelve other black messmen were below deck on the USS *West Virginia* preparing breakfast for the battleship's crew. They were talking and joking when they heard a loud explosion, quickly followed by several more explosions. The men exchanged puzzled looks. There must have been a terrible accident on a nearby ship, one of them guessed. They bounded up narrow steel stairs to the main deck.

Black smoke and yellow flames poured from battleships, cruisers, and destroyers anchored in the surrounding harbor. Japanese fighter planes, which Americans called Zeros, swarmed overhead like angry bees. One of the Zeros swooped down from the sky directly at the *West Virginia*. Its machine guns spewed bullets at sailors as they scurried to their battle stations, wearing only their underwear because they had been asleep in their bunks.

"Miller, give me a hand with the commander," someone shouted. "He's been hit." The muscular messman hurried over to where the ship's captain was lying in a pool of blood. He gathered the wounded commander in his arms and carried him below deck to safety.

The black sailor had not been trained for any duty other than kitchen work, but he returned to the ship's main deck and manned a large antiaircraft gun. He pointed at one of the Zeros speeding through the sky and began firing. To his surprise, the bullets ripped through the plane's fuselage. It spun out of control, burst into flames, and plunged into the ocean. In the next few minutes, Miller shot down four Zeros.

The sneak attack by two hundred Japanese fighter planes and bombers devastated Pearl Harbor. Two thousand

Battleships burning after the surprise attack on Pearl Harbor

Newspaper headline on December 8, 1941, the day the United States declared war against Japan

Americans were killed, eight battleships were sunk, and 188 airplanes were destroyed. In less than an hour, the U.S. Navy's Pacific fleet had been crippled.

The raid was part of Japan's plan to control the Pacific, just as their partners in war, the Germans, planned to control Europe. The Japanese army had already invaded China and Vietnam. Hoping to gain a military advantage, the Japanese attacked the United States, the only country strong enough to stop the aggressive nation. Four days after Pearl Harbor, Germany and Italy also declared war against the United States. America would have to fight powerful enemies in two very different parts of the world.

Remember Pearl Harbor became a popular slogan as stories about the bravery of American sailors during the attack filled newspapers and magazines. One of the few articles that mentioned African Americans referred only to a "Negro messman" who carried his wounded commander to safety.

The editors at the Pittsburgh *Courier* read the article and wanted to find the black hero whom the white press had not bothered to name. After a three-month search, they learned the messman was Dorie Miller, the twenty-two-year-old son of Texas sharecroppers. The newspaper printed several stories about the sailor, which prompted his commanders to award the messman their most prestigious medal for heroism, the Navy Cross. The young sailor was killed two years later on Thanksgiving Day when his ship was hit by a torpedo in the South Pacific.

Dorie Miller wearing his Navy Cross

Before Pearl Harbor, Messman Miller had been a typical black seaman. He was one of 4,000 African Americans among the 170,000 sailors in the U.S. Navy. This service allowed blacks to serve only as cooks, dishwashers, and busboys. They worked in the mess, which is military slang for dining room and kitchen. These sailors were simply seagoing servants. "Because men live in such intimacy aboard ship," an admiral explained, "we simply can't enlist Negroes above the rank of messmen." The Marine Corps, a division of the navy, had never allowed blacks to join its ranks.

In the largest branch of the armed forces, the army, there were fewer than 5,000 African Americans among the entire peacetime force of 230,000 soldiers. Most of them were segregated in four all-black units created after the Civil War, the Twenty-fourth and Twenty-fifth Infantry and the Ninth and Tenth Cavalry. There were only five black commissioned officers who were second lieutenants or higher in rank. The most prominent of the five was General Benjamin Davis. He became the first African American general when he was promoted in 1940. His son, Lieutenant Benjamin Davis Jr., another of the five officers, was one of only four blacks who had ever graduated from West Point.

The War Department, which was later renamed the Defense Department, estimated the armed forces needed at least eight million volunteers and draftees to fight both the Japanese and the Germans. These men had to be quickly inducted, trained, and dispatched to their assignments in Europe and the Pacific.

There were three million blacks among the thirty-one

The U.S. government used posters and other kinds of advertising to encourage Americans to work together to win the war.

million American men between the ages of eighteen and thirty-eight who registered with their Selective Service offices, popularly called draft boards. Every board was made up of citizens who selected local men for military service.

Black citizens sat on some draft boards in the North, but not on boards in the South, where most black Americans lived.

The majority of black men who were drafted served in the army, which insisted on segregating African American soldiers despite the objections of black leaders who wanted the armed forces to be integrated. "The settlement of vexing racial problems," said a general responding to these objections, "cannot be permitted to complicate the tremendous tasks of the War Department and thereby jeopardizing discipline and morale."

But segregation was itself a serious issue undermining army discipline and morale. Politicians, generals, and even the president were concerned with the problems of training and employing black soldiers.

The War Department tried to solve the problem by limiting the number of blacks in the armed forces to 10.6 percent of the total number of people in the military. This quota was chosen because it was the percentage of African Americans in the nation's population of 130 million. But the quota was hard to fill because so many blacks were rejected for military service.

The two main reasons for the high rejection rate were bad health, especially venereal diseases such as syphilis or gonorrhea, and illiteracy, the inability to read and write. Venereal disease could be cured with penicillin, but illiteracy was a tougher problem.

Early in the war, the army accepted only recruits with at least a fourth-grade education. So many men failed to meet this requirement that the army began accepting recruits with no education. Illiterate soldiers were sent to classes to learn basic reading and writing.

The decision to segregate African American soldiers also delayed induction while the army hastily constructed separate barracks, recreation halls, hospitals, and even separate ball fields. Blacks were often unhappy with their accommodations. They were assigned to barracks on the edge of camp, hundreds of yards from the post office, mess hall, and PX, or post exchange, which was like a convenience store. New recruits often arrived before buildings were finished. They had to move into barracks that lacked floors, screens, or windows. It was not unusual for fifty to one hundred men to live in barracks where buckets were their only latrines. The recreation halls for black soldiers were often too small for anything other than card games. White soldiers always had better barracks, better recreation halls, better everything.

The problems for African Americans were made worse because the army built many of its camps in the South, where short, mild winters allowed troops to train outdoors year round. White Southerners hated black soldiers, especially those from the North. And black soldiers who had grown up in such cities as Chicago, New York, or Philadelphia, where racial discrimination was less severe, hated white Southerners.

"To be a black soldier in the South in those days was one of the worst things that could happen to you," an African American explained. "If you go to town, you would have to get off the sidewalk if a white person came by. If you went into the wrong neighborhood wearing your uniform, you got beat up. If off post you was hungry and couldn't find a black restaurant or a black home . . . you would starve. And you were a soldier . . . out there wearing the uniform of your country, and you're getting treated like a dog!"

Many Southern towns asked the army not to send African American officers or Northern blacks to nearby bases. White Texans were especially wary because in World War I, black doughboys, angry after weeks of harassment by Houston police, marched into town and killed seventeen policemen, soldiers, and civilians. Despite local objections, the army stationed black GIs in every part of the country. Little was done, though, about the way civilians treated these men.

Soldiers enjoyed getting away from camp for a day to visit nearby towns. There was not much to do except stroll the streets, look in store windows, drink beer or Coca-Cola at a local restaurant, and, if they were lucky, talk to young women. But even these simple diversions were denied black army men.

Officials in some towns insisted African American GIs stay in black neighborhoods. If the soldiers were allowed on main street, shopkeepers frequently did not let them in their stores. Restaurants, when they served blacks at all, made them go to the back door or eat in the kitchen. "The white civilians hate us," complained a GI stationed in Texas. "They abuse us in any way they see fit."

One of the biggest problems was transportation. Public buses were the only way GIs could travel between their base and town. But a simple bus ride could be difficult. As one soldier recalled, "When we went to town on the bus, we had to get in the back, and if the bus was full—I mean full of whites—we had to wait until the next bus came. I've seen them [whites] just completely push the black soldiers off. We'd just wait in line for hours and hours."

Each day revealed new discrimination. The Red Cross even refused to accept blood donated by African Americans. The organization finally agreed to accept their blood, but it would not give plasma taken from a person of one race to a person of another race.

Blacks had little choice other than to endure the constant discrimination. But they occasionally struck back in small ways. Men from a tank battalion training at Ft. Hood, Texas, came across a sign in nearby Killeen that advised NIGGERS HAVE TO LEAVE THIS TOWN BY 9 PM.

"Well!" one of the soldiers recalled "I don't have to tell you what the tankers did. We tore that sign down and integrated another Southern town."

Resentment over army racism rose as the number of black GIs grew. There were a half million African Americans in the U.S. Army by the end of 1942. A GI stationed at an Army Air Force base in Texas summed up the anger felt by black soldiers. "Every Negro man on this post is absolutely fed up and disappointed with the bad treatment and discrimination, segregation and injustice imposed on us. . . . We are still slaves, laborers, and flunkies for the white personnel here. . . . We haven't had any drilling to speak of that could be classed as drilling. We had three weeks of basic training. It takes that long to learn to do the manual of arms (arms are something we haven't seen except a 45 on the MP's side, ready to blow your brains out if you resent being treated like a dog, or being called a nigger or a black son of a b———). . . . We are discriminated against in everything we do or take part in."

Such profound unhappiness, reported the army's chief of staff, had created "an immediate and serious problem among Negro troops." Fights, shootings, and riots between white soldiers and black soldiers were becoming commonplace.

Camp commanders prepared for race riots in the same matter-of-fact manner they prepared for fires. An army camp in Virginia kept a squad of riflemen on standby in case the three thousand black troops stationed there caused trouble. It was army policy at other camps that white soldiers outnumber black soldiers. But these precautions did not prevent serious incidents.

In Virginia, one hundred thirty black soldiers rioted because they were confined to the worst seats at a concert. There was a gun battle at Fort Stewart, Georgia, between military police, called MPs, and one hundred black soldiers. Four blacks had been wounded and one white MP killed by the time two battalions of soldiers in combat gear restored order.

Fights and riots did not happen just in the South. At Fort Dix, New Jersey, MPs and black GIs fought a gun battle after an argument erupted among soldiers waiting in line to use a public telephone. An MP and two soldiers were shot to death.

In the worst year of violence, 1943, there were incidents at dozens of military posts. Race riots involving civilians, soldiers, and sailors occurred in Los Angeles, Detroit, New York, and numerous other cities.

General Benjamin Davis blamed segregation for many of the problems. "The War Department is making no appreciable efforts to lessen the Jim Crow practices, which are by far the greatest factor on the morale of the colored soldier."

The War Department, yielding to demands from civil rights leaders, tried to reduce tension and improve morale among blacks by creating segregated combat infantry divisions that could go into battle against the Japanese and the Germans.

3

The First African American Combat Divisions

Black citizens were jubilant when they read that the old Ninety-second and Ninety-third Divisions, which had been the only two African American infantry divisions in World War I, were being reactivated for World War II. They felt it was important to serve, and even to die, in combat along with white Americans. "Prejudice and intolerance," said one black leader, "will have no place in the hearts and minds of comrades in arms who have fought and bled and conquered shoulder to shoulder."

The two divisions trained at Fort Huachuca, Arizona. This old outpost in southeast Arizona, near Mexico, had been built in 1877 and was named for the surrounding Huachuca Mountains. African American soldiers had been stationed at the fort since early in the century.

When the Ninety-third Division was activated there in early 1942, Fort Huachuca suddenly became the nation's largest, and only, predominately African American army post. The fort quickly grew from a sleepy outpost to a busy training camp of twenty-five thousand people. After the hasty construction of a thousand new buildings—everything from barracks to mess halls, fire stations, theaters, and churches—Fort Huachuca was big enough to be Arizona's third largest city.

The new recruits stationed there were in their teens and early twenties. These young men—some of them boys only fifteen or sixteen years old—arrived by train or bus from small towns and farms in faraway Virginia, North Carolina, Tennessee, and other states back East. Most of them had never been away from home before.

As soon as they arrived at Fort Huachuca, these men began learning how to be soldiers. Each morning before dawn, a bugler blew reveille to rouse them from their bunks. Then the recruits spent two hours jogging and doing sit-ups, push-ups, and other calisthenics. On some days, the new GIs went on long marches into the surrounding mountains, where Apache Indians once roamed. A company dressed for combat and carrying fifty-pound packs was expected to march twenty-five miles in eight hours or less.

The recruits learned survival techniques such as how to catch and eat snakes in case they were stranded in the jungle or forests. They were taught to read maps and to identify tanks and airplanes. The soldiers learned to spot land mines and booby traps, which an enemy might hide on a trail or road. The men practiced shooting and cleaning their rifles. And each GI took first-aid lessons so he could help himself or help other wounded soldiers on the battlefield.

Soldiers in World War II had to be better trained than in

Trainees doing calisthenics with their rifles

Soldiers at Fort Huachuca prepare for a long hike in the mountains.

previous wars because of all the modern weapons. Jeeps and tanks, flamethrowers and bazookas were used in that war for the first time. The most destructive new weapons were the B-52 bombers and the powerful explosives they dropped.

Fort Huachuca was the best army base in the United States for black GIs. The fort had a small, segregated hospital for white people, and a much larger hospital, with nearly one thousand beds, for African Americans. The large hospital's medical staff of over one hundred doctors and nurses was all black. Many of the soldiers, for the first time in their lives, had regular visits to doctors and dentists.

Prominent black civilians lavished attention on Fort Huachuca. Champion boxers Joe Louis and Sugar Ray Robinson gave exhibition matches during halftime at games in the fort's big football stadium. Celebrities such as Pearl Bailey, Lena Horne, and Louis Armstrong all gave concerts there. Horne, a beautiful actress and singer, visited so often she was crowned "Sweetheart of the Ninety-second Division."

There were only a few dozen nurses and two companies of the Women's Army Corps, known as WACs, stationed at Huachuca. The absence of women bothered some men, but others did not seem to mind. "Everyone had such a good time that the ladies were hardly missed," one GI commented after a Saturday night dance.

Soldiers seeking entertainment frequently visited Fry, the small civilian community near the fort. It was described as "an inferno of vice, wine, women, and jukeboxes." Black businessmen from Chicago wanted the GIs to have an alternative to the bars and brothels in this rough civilian community. They built a recreational hall dubbed the Green Top. It housed a dance hall, skating rink, shooting gallery, bar, and restaurant. The Green Top was popular, but it took little business from Fry's other bars. Nor did it hurt business for the hundreds of prostitutes who came to town on paydays to sell their services in the backseats of automobiles.

Soldiers spent their spare time on the base in reading rooms looking at popular newspapers or magazines. They also gathered around the radio to listen to music or news about the war. The radio had become popular in their life-time. It was still a novelty to sit by a little box listening to entertainers such as the Andrews Sisters singing their big wartime hit, "Don't Sit Under the Apple Tree with Anyone Else but Me."

Unlike black soldiers at other military camps, GIs at Huachuca had good athletic facilities. The men played a lot of baseball, football, and basketball. The fort named its base-ball diamond Foster Field in honor of Rube Foster, a famous pitcher and manager in Negro League baseball. The soldiers' first and only "Desert Bowl" football game was played on New Year's Day, 1943, in a stadium overflowing with four-teen thousand spectators.

While the facilities at Fort Huachuca were the best the army had to offer African Americans, discrimination still created serious problems. An African American complained that at officers' clubs, hospitals, guest quarters, and ball fields, whites "enforced the strictest segregation possible between themselves and the black officers. Their only contact was strictly in relation to military activities; social contact was out. How they could possibly function together in combat was a question that had to pass through many a black officer's mind, not to mention the minds of enlisted men."

Blacks also resented the fact that white officers were always in charge. The army believed that black enlisted men did not trust black officers. It also believed that the best leaders for African American soldiers were white Southerners who "understood Negroes." Hundreds of African Americans attended the same officer training schools that white men attended, but black officers were not allowed to command white GIs. "It gave overt sanction to theories that no Negro, no matter how competent," explained one African American, "could perform assigned duties better than any white man, no matter how incompetent."

Not surprisingly, black officers and white officers disliked one another. A soldier's letter to the Pittsburgh *Courier* listed a series of violent incidents at Fort Huachuca. "A white officer was beaten nearly to death one night. Somebody threw bricks through the commanding officer's car windows. Some Negro officers were mysteriously beaten."

Blacks often did not respect their commanders. "The majority of the white officers with the Ninety-third were people who could not have made it with any white division of any caliber," believed one black soldier. "They might have been all right in the quartermasters, or some laundry units. Instead of being sent to jobs they were fit for, they were sloughed off on the Ninety-third. I understand that what we didn't get of these misfits ended up with the Ninety-second Division."

White officers also had little faith in the men under their command. "I don't like my assignment because I don't trust Negroes," one officer explained. "White officers who work with them have to work harder than with white troops. I have no confidence in the fighting ability of Negro soldiers."

This officer's views were not entirely wrong. Many men in the black divisions were not good soldiers. The worst were those GIs classified as "Q-minus" or "Casuals" because mental, emotional, or physical problems kept them out of the regular training program. During its first year, the Ninety-third Division had to discharge four thousand of these men, one-fourth of its total.

For some of the enlisted men classified as Casuals or Q-minus, said one GI, their only problem was being in the "white man's" army. "We put every bit of our brain power together in the art of evading, dodging, and lying, if caught. However, we're very careful to make sure the 'great white father' was unaware that we're goofing off three-quarters of the time."

Under different conditions these men might have made good GIs. "The only sickness those Casuals had was one of morale," observed a black officer. "If they had been treated as human beings, as soldiers in the United States Army, they would not have become a problem."

The army recognized that these problems had been

caused by African Americans growing up in segregated, poor communities. They "came into the army with fewer educational and cultural opportunities," observed Major Paul Goodman of the Ninety-second Division, "and came from homes with lower socioeconomic status than men in other divisions." Major Goodman could have added that many years of segregation had created a wide gulf of misunderstanding and distrust between black Americans and white Americans that kept them from working together to defend their nation. Despite the recognition of the problem, there was little the army could do to remedy it quickly.

Men of the 93rd snug in their bunks on a ship sailing to the South Pacific

Poor leadership dampened the morale of the two combat divisions. The best soldiers often transferred to other posts. "I began to have misgivings about following this kind of officer into battle, and I became determined to get out of the Ninety-second," explained a soldier who joined a paratrooper regiment and rose to the rank of lieutenant colonel. The problems caused by bad officers and poorly motivated men plagued the two black infantry divisions for the entire war.

Both divisions completed a year of basic training at Fort Huachuca. The first to finish was the Ninety-third. In the spring of 1943, the whole division left Arizona on seventy-two trains. It traveled to the swamps of southern Louisiana for several months of advanced training in jungle warfare. Then the division shipped out across the Pacific Ocean to meet the Japanese.

4

Fighting the Japanese

American forces were fighting their way, island by island, across the ocean to Japan in early 1944 when the Ninety-third Infantry Division arrived in the South Pacific.

After Pearl Harbor, the Japanese had quickly captured the Philippines and several other Pacific islands. They were poised to attack Australia when the tides of war changed. Starting with the two-day naval Battle of the Coral Sea in May 1942, the Americans began to turn the Japanese back. A month later, the U.S. Navy sank four enemy battleships and won the great Battle of the Midway Islands. The marines endured six months of savage fighting and enormous casualties before winning another important victory on Guadalcanal.

The Ninety-third Division was divided between two very different assignments. Two-thirds of the men were sent to the New Georgia Islands, where they guarded airfields and worked in the ports. This was the same kind of work performed by most of the other two hundred thousand African American soldiers stationed on islands in the Pacific Ocean.

The division's remaining five thousand men were shipped to a battle zone on Bougainville, the largest of the Solomon Islands.

The black soldiers joined other American troops holding a beachhead at the southern end of the 125-mile long island. Most of Bougainville was occupied by an estimated twenty-five thousand Japanese soldiers. Just two weeks earlier, these enemy troops had attempted unsuccessfully to drive the GIs into the sea. The failed attack left the enemy isolated and discouraged. The main job for the Americans was to keep supplies from reaching the Japanese so they would either surrender or starve to death.

After two weeks of learning about jungle fighting with experienced outfits, the newcomers were sent into combat. A battalion, which is made up of several companies, was ordered to destroy enemy detachments guarding the Laruam River. To surprise their foes, the men, armed with mortars and machine guns, descended a sixty-foot bluff by rope. A squad of GIs waded across the river, but they were immediately pinned down by fierce machine-gun fire from a cluster of pillboxes.

Private Wade Foggie braved enemy bullets to set up a rocket launcher and then fired eight explosive rockets into the pillboxes. They destroyed the machine guns and killed ten enemy soldiers. Foggie was awarded the Ninety-third Division's first Bronze Star for heroism.

White commanders closely watched the black soldiers. According to most reports, the newcomers performed their assignments satisfactorily. They also got along reasonably

Soldiers from the 93rd on patrol in the Bougainville jungle

Infantrymen cross a river. Some of the men carry artillery shells.

well with the white troops. The men of the Ninety-third were glad to be on the battlefront, and their morale was good. Everything was okay until the Company K affair.

Company K, under the command of a white captain, James J. Curran, went on its first patrol only two weeks after arriving on the island. The company, which consisted of three platoons, was followed by a photographer and a reporter preparing newspaper articles about the black soldiers.

The men of Company K were excited to be on their first patrol. They walked in single file, quietly and expectantly, along the jungle trail. It was shaded by the dense growth of trees and leafy plants, which prevented the GIs from seeing more than a few yards in any direction. After a half mile, they came across a cluster of bamboo huts once used as a Japanese hospital. Captain Curran ordered a dozen men to follow the trail beyond the huts to scout for enemy soldiers. Soon after the scouting party had disappeared into the jungle, several rifle shots rang out. One of the scouts yelled back that they had spotted three "Japs" and killed two of them.

Accompanied by a sergeant and two privates, Captain Curran went to investigate. They had gone only a few yards when rifle shots from the jungle felled the two privates. The captain shouted for the others to spread out to avoid being easy targets. Instead, the frightened men crowded together. Then, without orders, the soldiers started shooting wildly into the jungle. The captain yelled for them to stop. He knew the wild shots might hit his GIs up ahead on the trail.

Captain Curran told his men to pick up the wounded and to start an orderly withdrawal, one platoon at a time. The sergeant in charge of the First Platoon threw off his pack, dropped his rifle, and ran. The rest of his platoon quickly followed.

Seeing the First Platoon disappear down the trail, the remaining soldiers became even more frightened and clustered around their captain. He ordered them to withdraw, a few at a time. The men would not obey orders to stop shooting. They fired at any bush that moved. The only

GIs aiding a wounded soldier

one among them with combat experience, a sergeant, tried to reassure the scared GIs. "He walked calmly up and down carrying his carbine," the newspaper reporter recalled, "telling the men there was nothing to worry about, that there were a few Japs, and that if they held, everything would turn out OK."

Despite the frightening confusion, other GIs acted bravely too. Oscar Davenport, a black lieutenant, remained behind until all able-bodied men in his platoon had withdrawn. Then, under fire, Lieutenant Davenport began crawling over to aid a wounded soldier. He was immediately hit by a bullet. Ignoring his own wound, Davenport kept crawling toward the fallen soldier. Just as he reached the wounded man, the lieutenant was shot again and killed.

The skirmish lasted a half hour. When it stopped, ten Americans had been killed and twenty wounded. No one knew how many had been hit by so-called friendly fire, the wild shooting of their comrades. The other GIs returned to the safety of their own lines. Some claimed to have been jumped by a whole Japanese regiment, although none of them actually saw more than three enemy soldiers.

Experienced battlefield officers were not surprised that new troops would panic under fire; it happened often. An official investigation of the incident later concluded that Company K had been poorly trained.

Much more damning than the official reports were the two very different versions of the incident spreading among servicemen throughout the Pacific. Black troops said the white captain ran away while the black officer, Lieutenant

Davenport, sacrificed his life trying to lead his men to safety. The whole affair, African Americans believed, was covered up to avoid punishing white officers.

White soldiers told a much different story. They said that blacks ran from the fighting, which caused many white GIs to be killed. One general asserted, "Colored boys just wouldn't fight."

The Ninety-third was never assigned to combat duty again. For the rest of the war, the division worked at a variety of tasks on Bougainville and on other islands. It loaded and unloaded ships, guarded airfields, and hunted small bands of Japanese resisters hiding in the jungle. There were some proud moments. A black outfit captured an enemy colonel, one of the highest-ranking Japanese officers taken prisoner in the entire war. Japanese officers usually killed themselves rather than be captured.

While the Ninety-third Division finished the war behind the front lines in the Pacific, halfway around the world, in Europe, the Allies needed every available soldier to battle the Germans in both France and Italy.

5

The Normandy Invasion

The German soldiers who were hunkered down in concrete bunkers with their machine guns pointed toward Great Britain first heard the noise before dawn. As the sound grew louder, they recognized the drone of hundreds of low-flying airplanes. These young soldiers knew something horrific was coming. Their skin tingled as they peered into the dark for a glimpse of the invading enemy.

Suddenly, they saw a bright flash. It was quickly followed by more flashes, like lightning on the horizon. Then the storm broke with a fury few men ever experience. The earth shook as shell after shell fired from offshore destroyers and battleships slammed into the beach. Airplanes, artillery fire, and exploding bombs created a wall of deafening noise.

D-Day, the biggest amphibian military invasion in the history of the world, began shortly after midnight on June 6, 1944. Some 500 black soldiers were among the 130,000 British, Canadian, and American troops who waded ashore that morning onto five beaches along a fifty-mile strip of French coast. The British and Canadians stormed three beaches with code names Gold, Juno, and Sword. The Americans stormed Utah and Omaha beaches, where the heaviest fighting occurred. The African Americans were members of the 320th Barrage Balloon Battalion. Under heavy enemy fire, the 320th set up a protective screen of large balloons to obscure the soldiers on Utah and Omaha beaches from German warplanes.

The Normandy invasion lasted three weeks. During that time, some 4,000 ships transported 850,000 soldiers from England to German-occupied France. They brought with them 150,000 tanks, jeeps, and trucks, as well as 500,000

Ships, part of the D-Day invasion force, unloading hundreds of trucks, carry supplies for the invading Allies.

tons of food, ammunition, medicine, and other supplies.

The Allies had prepared for the D-Day invasion for nearly two years in Great Britain, less than one hundred miles across the English Channel from France. The 3 million soldiers stationed there included 154,000 black GIs. British officials had asked the United States not to send African American soldiers. They did not want racial conflict added to the problems they already expected from millions of soldiers in their small nation. Great Britain, which consists of Ireland, Scotland, Wales, and England, is no larger than New York State. The English summed up their feelings about American soldiers by joking, "They're overfed, oversexed, and over here."

Every available man was needed to prepare for the invasion of German-occupied France, so the United States did not honor Britain's request. More African Americans were sent to Great Britain during the war than to any other country. British civilians greeted black GIs with warmth and respect. But, as the British had feared, racial conflict would become a serious problem.

African American GIs in England told a black reporter that they felt white Americans were their enemies. "You cannot believe the lies [white GIs] have told about us," one soldier complained. "They try to keep us out of all the pubs, and when they can't, they fight us. The MPs lock us up, especially if they see us talking with any English women. They go in gangs and beat you up, and then if our boys have to cut some of them to keep from getting hurt, they say Negro soldiers are bad."

In their letters home, white soldiers expressed surprise that British civilians were friendly with African Americans. They especially hated to see English women dating black men. "Every time we have seen a nigger with a white girl we have run him away," one GI wrote. "I would like to shoot the whole bunch of them." Interracial dating was such an emotional subject that the War Department prohibited U.S. magazines and newspapers from publishing photographs "showing Negro soldiers in poses of intimacy with white women or conveying 'boyfriend-girlfriend' implications."

General Dwight D. Eisenhower, the Supreme Allied

General Dwight D. Eisenhower talks with a GI. Seven years after World War II ended, General Eisenhower was elected president of the United States.

Commander of Allied Forces in Europe, expected trouble between white GIs and black GIs. He issued a strong warning to base commanders to make sure African American soldiers were treated fairly.

Among the Americans sent to England was the only black battalion of the Women's Army Corps to serve overseas. There were only 4,000 African American WACs in the whole army, and 855 of them belonged to the 6888th Central Postal Directory Battalion. These women were sent to England to sort and deliver army mail. It was a large, complicated, and, before the arrival of the 6888th, backed-up postal system. In a few weeks, the women had the system operating smoothly.

After the Allies landed in Normandy, some fifty thousand African Americans were shipped across the English Channel to France. They were among the hundreds of thousands of soldiers who belonged to port battalions, truck companies, engineering, and other noncombat outfits. These men delivered supplies, set up camps, and repaired roads. Although they received less attention than combat troops, their work was essential. An army without gasoline or bullets or food would be quickly defeated.

One of the most famous supply operations was the Red Ball Express. Army trucks sped over a long highway, carrying food and ammunition from the coast to the Allied invasion force advancing rapidly against the Germans near Paris. The men, many of whom were black, drove thirty-six-hour shifts without rest. Their trucks ran twenty-two hours, with only a two-hour stop for mechanics to check tires, oil,

WACs of the 6888th Central Postal Directory Battalion in France

and engines. They maintained this pace for twelve days over war-torn roads. The trucks were frequently shelled by enemy artillery or strafed by fighter planes. During these twelve days, the trucks used 300,000 gallons of gasoline while delivering 90,000 tons of supplies.

Twenty-two black units, mostly artillery, tank, and engineer companies, participated in the drive across France. They included the 761st Tank Battalion, nicknamed the Black Panthers.

The 761st was under the command of one of America's most brilliant commanders, General George Patton. The general welcomed the battalion's seven hundred soldiers to his command with a short speech. "Men, you're the first Negro tankers to ever fight in the American army. I would never have asked for you if you weren't good. I have nothing but the best in my army. I don't care what color you are, so long as you go up there and kill those Kraut sonsabitches. Everyone has their eyes on you and is expecting great things from you. Most of all, your race is looking to you. Don't let them down, don't let me down." The 761st did not let anyone down. It compiled a distinguished combat record while fighting for 183 consecutive days without relief.

While the Black Panthers were helping push the Nazis out of France, the Ninety-second Infantry Division had traveled from Fort Huachuca to the Italian front, where it was the only complete African American infantry division to go into battle.

6

The Ninety-second Infantry Division in Italy

Hundreds of black army stevedores noisily cheered and waved when the Ninety-second Division arrived on the docks at Naples, Italy, in July 1944. In the crowd were reporters and photographers from American newspapers and magazines. They were writing articles on the first black American infantrymen in Europe. Even General Benjamin Davis was there with a film crew making a documentary film called *Teamwork*. Over the next few weeks, other prominent leaders—including Winston Churchill, Great Britain's prime minister—visited the soldiers.

The GIs getting all of the attention were a carefully selected combat team, nicknamed the Raiders, composed of the Ninety-second Division's best soldiers. They were assigned to the U.S. Fifth Army which, along with the British Eighth Army, was trying to drive the Germans out of Italy.

A year earlier, the Allies had invaded the southern part of the boot-shaped Italian peninsula, which is nearly eight hundred miles long and about twice the size of Florida. They had hoped to defeat the Germans and their Italian supporters within just a few months, but the enemy was well prepared for the invasion.

When the Raiders arrived in Naples, there were twenty-three divisions of Nazi soldiers in the Apennine Mountains. These steep mountains were a rugged, natural fortress one hundred fifty miles north of Rome, Italy's ancient capital. The Germans, who had orders from Hitler to defend the Apennines to the last man, had dug bunkers beneath the stone on the mountaintops to protect their men from air attacks. Long-range artillery prevented Allied soldiers from venturing up the narrow Alpine passes. To reach the Germans in their rocky fortresses, the Allies would have to climb bare hills while dodging machine-gun and mortar fire.

These Nazi defenses, stretching across the top of Italy, were called the Gothic Line. The Allies wanted to break through this line to reach Germany, on the other side of the mountains.

The Raiders were assigned a position just south of the Gothic Line, along the Ligurian Sea on Italy's west coast. The autumn weather was good and enemy resistance was light. The men from the Ninety-second skirmished several times with the Nazis. In those first few weeks, 8 African Americans were killed, 248 were sick or wounded, and 23 were missing or captured.

The black soldiers fought their first big battle in early October. They were ordered to attack artillery placements on Mount Cauala, a steep hill guarding Highway One, the

GIs advancing on the Germans in the rugged mountains of northern Italy

main road along the Italian west coast. It was necessary to knock out these enemy guns so that Allied tanks and soldiers could travel up Highway One to capture the city of Massa.

The Raiders advanced across a narrow plain dotted by marshes and crisscrossed by canals and streams. Then they slowly climbed to the top of Mount Cauala. Near the crest, the GIs were surprised by heavy fire from machine guns, rifles, and mortars. Four hundred men were quickly killed or wounded. The sudden, fierce attack caused confusion and panic among the Americans. They fled down the hill for the safety of a nearby town. Retreating without orders was a serious breech of military discipline. If there had not been a shortage of infantrymen, the Raiders might have been reassigned to jobs unloading ships or driving trucks.

The rest of the Ninety-second Infantry Division, some twelve thousand men, arrived in October. By December, the entire division was guarding twenty-two miles of the front and engaging in numerous small fights with the enemy. Some black GIs were shirkers; most simply tried to do their jobs while staying alive; and a few proved to be courageous. The bravery of one lieutenant in the hillside village of Sommocolonia was especially memorable.

One night, small groups of Italians began drifting into town. The Americans occupying the town assumed they were local residents and therefore harmless. They proved to be Fascists, Italians who sided with the Nazis. The following morning, the Fascists began shooting GIs just as German soldiers began to attack.

Badly outnumbered, Lieutenant John R. Fox and three dozen of his men took shelter in a house. Lieutenant Fox got on the radio and ordered an artillery barrage on the town. When the enemy began closing in, the lieutenant shouted into the radio for the big guns to immediately begin shelling the house. At first, the men in the artillery battalion refused, but Lieutenant Fox insisted. When the Allies recaptured the town, they found the bodies of the lieutenant and his men in the rubble of the house. Nearby were an estimated one hundred dead German soldiers.

The entire Ninety-second Division launched its first big attack, with the code name Operation Fourth Term, in early February. The attack began in the morning with airplanes strafing and bombing German bunkers guarding the highway to Massa. Next, hundreds of tanks and some twelve thousand infantrymen began their slow advance against the enemy.

One objective was to capture three hills with the code names X, Y, and Z. The hills were as high as hundred-story buildings. There were few trees or shrubs to shield the men.

As the GIs carefully advanced up the side of Hill X, they were accidentally strafed by an Allied fighter plane. It killed or wounded a dozen men. The attack was discouraging, yet the Ninety-second pushed ahead and captured Hill X. They held it for six hours, until a heavy artillery barrage and the threat of a German counterattack caused them to panic. The men quickly retreated down the hill, looking for safety. Many of them hid in farmhouses or caves. Special units searched the countryside, rounding up thousands of stragglers. After four days of fighting and heavy losses, the infantrymen ended where they had started, on the plain looking up at the Germans on Hills X, Y, and Z.

The worst fighting during the four-day battle occurred on a seaside beach where a company of tanks, with engineers and infantrymen riding on top, had to cross a canal. On the opposite side, the infantrymen would protect the engineers while they cleared the beach of mines so the tanks could drive ashore.

About halfway across the shallow canal, the lead tank struck a mine. The explosion crippled the vehicle, forcing the tanks following behind to stop. Then, German artillery shells began raining down on the Americans. "The first one hit squarely in the middle of my little command group," one of the officers recalled, "and when I looked around, there were only two others who had not been hit. The shell had killed seven. The entire mouth of the canal appeared to turn red with blood."

By the second day, a few soldiers had managed to cross the canal. But it was a difficult position to hold. While digging foxholes in the beach, several men were killed when their shovels struck land mines. By this time, fewer than one hundred GIs were still fighting. Others were wounded or dead, but the majority had fled. There was no hope of reinforcements arriving quickly. The company commander decided to withdraw.

In the four-day attack, 47 officers and 657 enlisted men from the Ninety-second were killed, wounded, or missing in action. Twenty-four tanks were destroyed. They also lost many rifles and ammunition, which deserters had tossed aside.

Desertion in battle is a serious offense. The Fifth Army's commanders searched for answers as to why black troops seemed to "melt away" in battle. There were at least two explanations for the failure. One was that they did not trust their white commanders. "The men don't feel their officers are fit to lead them into combat," one report concluded.

The second explanation was that too many unmotivated and poorly trained soldiers were concentrated in the Ninety-second Division. White GIs who were not good soldiers could be spread among numerous divisions, but black infantrymen could be assigned only to the Ninety-second or Ninety-third Divisions. This meant that bad soldiers were grouped together and hurt the performance of the whole division.

Just before the February battle, the Ninety-second had received two thousand former quartermaster troops as infantry replacements. These men had been truck drivers, supply clerks, and stevedores, and only a few of them were given refresher courses in combat training before they were sent into battle. "There are few men in active combat who do not know the meaning of fear," one commander remarked. "The poorer trained the troops and the less experience they have had in fighting together, the greater degree of fear they realize."

Fifth Army headquarters reorganized the division to make it an effective fighting force in time for the next major attack. After the reorganization, the Ninety-second had three infantry regiments. The only remaining African American regiment was the 370th. Two others had been added. They were the 442nd, which was Japanese American, and the 473rd, which was white American. Both of the new regiments had extensive combat experience. The 442nd, in fact, was the most decorated group of men in the U.S. Army.

The reorganization was completed by April, just in time for Operation Second Wind, the code name for the last big Allied offensive in Italy. Tens of thousands of British and

The 442nd Regimental Combat Team, an outfit of Japanese Americans, joined the 92nd in the final drive against the German army in northern Italy.

American soldiers attacked the Gothic Line. The Ninety-second's mission was to silence the artillery guarding Highway One and then capture the city of Massa.

Captain John F. Runyon, the white commander of Company C of the 370th Infantry, provided an account of his company's role in the offensive. Company C had 142 black enlisted men, 1 black officer, and 3 white officers. These men assembled for battle after midnight of April 5. It was a cold night with a clear sky full of stars.

Captain Runyon gave his men a pep talk. The Ninety-second had not been fighting well, he told them, but this time they needed to "bring credit to Negroes in combat." Captain Runyon later recalled that "the men knew they had a real job to do, and they seemed determined to make good."

Their assignment was to capture an old hilltop castle that the Germans had turned into a fortress. The company advanced up the hill "on the run." Captain Runyon remembered the fear that gripped everyone. "I spied a group from our mortar section. They were on bended knees, praying. An enemy machine gun was firing over them."

The Americans advanced so quickly that they were on top of a German bunker before the enemy could fire their machine guns. Both sides began shooting at almost point-blank range. In fierce hand-to-hand combat, soldiers lunged at each other with bayonets, used their rifles as clubs, and gouged and kicked wildly.

The GIs overwhelmed the Nazis in the bunker, but they could go no farther because of heavy rifle and machine-gun fire from the castle. Over half of Company C already had been wounded or killed. Captain Runyon radioed for reinforcements. He was told that stubborn enemy resistance was keeping other companies from advancing. The captain knew his men would not survive an enemy counterattack, so he ordered Company C to withdraw.

Hearing that order, Second Lieutenant Vernon Joseph Baker, the only black officer, broke into tears. "Captain, we can't withdraw," he pleaded. "We must stay here and fight it out."

"I knew Lieutenant Baker desperately wanted these men of C Company to hold their ground," Captain Runyon later recalled, "and he was willing to sacrifice his own life in an effort to win our battle." The lieutenant had already fought heroically, having destroyed a German observation post and machine-gun nest.

During the retreat, Lieutenant Baker aided his troops by exposing himself to the enemy and drawing their fire. This diversion gave the Americans, especially those soldiers carrying wounded GIs, an opportunity to safely pull back. Baker had another opportunity to display his bravery when two machine guns pinned the company down as it was trying to withdraw. The lieutenant risked his life by crawling up to each of the machine-gun positions and destroying them with grenades. Company C then continued its withdrawal down the mountain.

But Lieutenant Baker was not finished. The following night he voluntarily led a mission through minefields. This extraordinary soldier was awarded a Distinguished Service

Cross, America's second highest military honor. He was the only officer in the Ninety-second to win that medal.

The main thrust of the division's attack was led by the battle-hardened 442nd. These Japanese American GIs had the toughest assignment. At night, they climbed up twenty-five hundred feet of unfamiliar rocky ground to surprise the enemy at daybreak. The 442nd then went on to capture Mount Brugiano north of Massa and successfully block the retreat of the Germans from the city. The Ninety-second rounded up thousands of German prisoners.

The city was captured by the 758th and 760th Tank Battalions, which charged up Highway One through tank traps, mines, mortars, and heavy artillery. At the edge of Massa, the tankers ran into heavy resistance from German machine-gun nests and snipers. The tank battalions, which were accompanied by infantrymen, slowly fought their way to the center of town, and enemy resistance collapsed.

By the end of April, the Allies had broken the Gothic Line and captured the major cities of northern Italy. The Nazis had put up stiff resistance, but they were unwilling to die holding their ground because they knew the war was almost over.

General Eisenhower's men had pushed Hitler's army out of France. The Allies were invading Germany, and African American volunteers were in the front of this final drive to win the war.

7

Equality on the Battlefield

On December 26, General Eisenhower's headquarters distributed an urgent message to all service battalions—the truck drivers and the supply clerks—asking African Americans to volunteer to fight at the front. A horrific battle had been raging fourteen days. Casualties were heavy. More men were needed.

Three hundred thousand German soldiers had surprised the Allies as they were advancing across Belgium. It was the biggest Nazi offensive of the war. The sudden and forceful counterattack shoved American forces back sixty-five miles. This created a huge bulge in the middle of the Allied line, which gave the engagement its name, the Battle of the Bulge.

Among the few black soldiers who were directly involved in the fighting were two artillery companies, the 333rd and 969th. They helped successfully defend the city of Bastogne, an important Allied communication and transportation center. The 969th's artillerymen picked up the rifles of dead soldiers and fought beside the all-white 101st Airborne Division.

Some 600,000 American soldiers were in the Battle of the Bulge. The casualties were enormous. Over 20,000 Americans were killed, and 40,000 were wounded. In just one engagement, the Germans took 7,000 prisoners. Overall, the Nazis captured 20,000 Allied troops and destroyed 800 tanks.

The large number of casualties made Eisenhower decide to ask black service troops to volunteer for frontline combat

German soldiers advance rapidly against the Allies during the Battle of the Bulge.

duty. They would be sent "without regard to color or race to the units where assistance is most needed." Black GIs and white GIs would fight "shoulder to shoulder to bring about victory." But the urgency of battle proved secondary to the politics of race.

The proposal to assign individual black soldiers to white outfits, one general complained, was "a clear invitation to embarrassment to the War Department." And, he added, it was "the most dangerous thing in regard to Negro relations." Eisenhower heeded the general's concern and rewrote the order to specify that volunteers would serve only in all-black platoons commanded by white men.

The response was overwhelming. More than forty-five hundred black soldiers, most from transportation or engineering companies, offered to give up their relatively safe jobs to go into battle. Nearly half of these men had to be turned down because all of them could not be trained quickly enough. The volunteers even included numerous officers who had to give up their commissions so they would not outrank white officers in their new companies.

From the very beginning, the black volunteers inspired confidence. "These men will fight because they have been trained and treated just like the other soldiers here," reported the colonel in charge of the training center where the volunteers spent six weeks. "And they know they are going to be used in the same manner in the same divisions. They want to fight. When the first group went out, we had only two cases of AWOL among all the Negro soldiers in the center. We found out where these two men were when we received a wire from a frontline division commander informing us that they had reported to him to fight."

The volunteers created fifty-three platoons. They did not finish their training in time for the Battle of the Bulge, which the Allies had won by the end of February. But the black soldiers were ready for combat just in time for the final Allied thrust into the heart of Germany. Some black soldiers, like the two who went AWOL, were criticized for being "overeager and too aggressive," which caused many of them to be wounded or killed. But that aggressiveness also proved valuable in battle.

When an American squadron scouting a German town was surrounded and in danger of being destroyed, two tank platoons accompanied by black infantrymen came to the rescue. The big steel tanks thundered into town, but they were immediately stopped by heavy German artillery fire. Four tanks were damaged and two were destroyed. The others quickly pulled back out of range of the enemy guns. The infantrymen who had been following behind the tanks took over. They fought their way from building to building until every German soldier had been killed or captured.

Black soldiers demonstrated their enthusiasm for battle again when a tank battalion advancing on a town in another part of Germany was ambushed. African American infantrymen were riding on top of the tanks. Sergeant Edward Allen Carter Jr. jumped to the ground and ordered three other GIs to follow him. They were going to attack the Nazis who were firing on them from a clump of trees on the other side of an open field.

A few of the volunteers for the final drive into Germany

Two former officers practice their marksmanship before heading for the front.

Grim-faced GIs receiving instructions before going into battle

A tank crew takes on ammunition. The crew ignores the decomposing German soldier in the foreground.

Soldiers gather the dead after a battle.

Crouching low to avoid enemy gunfire, Sergeant Carter led the way. They had gone only a short distance before all three of his men were hit. Two were killed, and the third was badly wounded. The sergeant continued alone, seemingly unconcerned with the bullets zipping by him. He was struck five times. As Carter lay on the ground, eight German soldiers emerged from the woods and sprinted across the field, intent on capturing the wounded American.

Sergeant Carter lay very still as the Germans approached. When they were within a few feet, he raised himself up and began shooting, hitting six of them. The other two immediately threw down their guns and surrendered. Using the enemy soldiers as shields, Carter retraced his steps to

By April of 1945, victory was certain, and these artillerymen displayed some humor.

the safety of the tank batallion. The prisoners revealed useful information on the strength and location of their troops. For his bravery, Sergeant Carter was awarded the Distinguished Service Cross.

The African Americans who volunteered for combat proved something else beyond the fact that black soldiers in battle could be as brave as anyone. They proved that white soldiers and black soldiers could get along and fight effectively together.

One officer reported on this "experiment" two months after a black platoon had been assigned to his company. "There has never appeared the slightest sign of race preju-

An infantryman with Nazi prisoners

dice or discrimination in this organization. White men and black men are welded together with a deep friendship and respect born of combat and matured by a realization that such an association is not the impossibility that many of us have been led to believe. Segregation has never been attempted in this unit and is, in my mind, the deciding factor as to the success or failure of the experiment. . . . My men eat, play, work, and sleep as a company of men, with no regard to color."

GIs move cautiously through the streets of a bombed-out German city.

On May 8, Germany officially surrendered. After VE Day, or Victory in Europe Day, the volunteer infantrymen were sent back to their original companies. Their disappointment was visible. "These colored men cannot understand why they are not being allowed to share the honor of returning to their homeland with the division in which they fought," one white officer noted, "proving to the world that Negro soldiers can do something besides drive a truck or work in a laundry."

The United States fought the Japanese for nearly four more months. That Asian nation finally surrendered in mid-August, soon after the United States dropped atomic bombs on the cities of Hiroshima and Nagasaki, killing or wounding a quarter of a million civilians. World War II—the greatest war in the history of mankind—was over. Millions of American servicemen and women eagerly returned home. One victory—half of the Double V Campaign—had been won, but there would be many more battles to fight before the second victory.

8

One More Victory To Win

Black soldiers returned to the United States and joined other African Americans in the second part of the Double V Campaign, fighting racism. It took years of blood and tears, but legal segregation was finally banished as an accepted feature of American life. People then began trying to correct the long legacy of injustice.

This legacy included the fact that there were no blacks among the 433 servicemen in World War II who received the Medal of Honor, America's highest award. A special investigation a half-century later found that African Americans were not awarded the medal because of the "climate of racial prejudice" during the 1940s. On January 13, 1997, President Bill Clinton bestowed the Medal of Honor on seven black men. All of them had risked or sacrificed their lives to save others. Six of these soldiers were infantrymen or tankers.

The one exception was George Watson of Birmingham, Alabama. He was a private in the Twenty-ninth Quartermaster Regiment. His ship, a transport, was sunk by the Japanese near New Guinea in March 1943. Instead of seeking safety, Watson remained in the water helping rescue men who could not swim. The exertion left him so weak that Watson was unable to save himself, and he drowned.

Two of the Medal of Honor winners had served with tank battalions. Edward Allen Carter Jr. of Los Angeles, California, was the aggressive African American soldier who was wounded five times yet managed to capture two prisoners during the final thrust into Germany. The second was Ruben Rivers of Oklahoma City, Oklahoma. He was a staff sergeant with the famed 761st Tank Battalion. While advancing across France, his tank ran over a land mine, and he was seriously wounded. Sergeant Rivers, refusing treatment, took command of another tank, and for three days he led his squad during a fierce battle. He died in that battle when his tank was destroyed by a German tank.

The highest-ranking African American to win the medal was Major Charles L. Thomas of Detroit, Michigan. In the fall of 1944, while advancing through northern France, the scout car Thomas was riding in was hit by enemy artillery. Major Thomas was severely wounded, but he helped his crew to safety. Then he managed to alert the column of American soldiers on the road behind him of the danger, which prevented numerous casualties. Thomas refused evacuation until he knew his junior officer was in control.

Private Willy F. James Jr. of Kansas City, Missouri, earned his Medal of Honor during the invasion of Germany. He volunteered to scout enemy positions while under intense fire. James returned to his unit, helped plan the attack, and then led the attack. He was killed by machine-gun fire while trying to rescue his wounded platoon leader.

Two African Americans who served with the Ninety-second Division in Italy received Medals of Honor. One was First Lieutenant John R. Fox of Cincinnati, Ohio. He was the soldier in Sommocolonia who died when, surrounded by the enemy, he called for artillery fire on his own position.

The other was Second Lieutenant Vernon Joseph Baker of St. Maries, Idaho. He had risked his life helping C Company withdraw from Hill X. Baker, at age seventy-seven, was the only one of the seven veterans still living.

President Bill Clinton awarded the Medal of Honor to Vernon J. Baker and six other African American soldiers for their exceptional bravery during World War II.

"It's a great day," Baker commented during the award ceremony at the White House. "The only thing I can say to those who were not here with me today is: 'Thank you, fellows. Well done. I'll always remember you.'"

The Medal of Honor awards were one more achievement in the long struggle for Double V. These soldiers fought and died for victory abroad. At home, the second victory has taken longer. But the White House ceremony proved that African Americans were slowly winning the recognition and rights other Americans have long enjoyed.

Gallery of Firsts

World War II was a time of rapid change for all Americans. The urgent need for manpower during the war removed some of the barriers of segregation. Black men and women were assigned jobs and responsibilities previously denied them because of their color. The following African Americans were among the first to assume those new responsibilities.

Benjamin O. Davis was the first black American general.

Dorie Miller, the first African American awarded the Navy Cross, was among the first blacks assigned to help recruit men for the navy.

The Tuskegee Airmen were the army air force's first black combat pilots. The many books and films about these men have made them the best-known black soldiers of World War II. They were called Tuskegee Airmen because they trained at a segregated base in Tuskegee, Alabama.

Black soldiers were assigned to tank battalions for the first time in World War II. The most famous was the 761st Tank Battalion, the only all-black outfit to win a Presidential Unit Citation.

During the war, women of all races took over jobs that had been traditionally performed by men. These WACs at Fort Huachuca, Arizona, were mechanics.

Mary McLeod Bethune, on the left, a prominent educator and civil rights activist, was Director of Negro Affairs in the National Youth Administration. She was the first black woman appointed to a high-level government job. Bethune used her influence with President Franklin D. Roosevelt to get better treatment for black men and women in the armed forces.

Howard D. Perry was the first black marine in that service's 167-year history. The marines began accepting African Americans June 1, 1942.

Colonel Benjamin O. Davis Jr. was the first black officer given command of an army post. In 1945, he took over Godman Air Field in Kentucky.

African Americans were admitted to all branches of the navy for the first time in 1942. The USS Mason, *the first ship in the navy to have a predominantly black crew, was commissioned in 1944. Later that year, the 160 men on the ship were recommended for letters of commendation for their bravery while guiding a convoy safely through ninety-mile-an-hour winds and forty-foot waves. The recommendation was misplaced, deliberately some suspect, for fifty years. Twelve crew members finally received their letters of commendation on February 16, 1995.*

Significant Events

1939 Germany invades Poland, September 1.

Two days after the invasion of Poland, England and France, which had pledged to defend the smaller nation, declare war on Germany; World War II begins.

1940 Benjamin O. Davis Sr. becomes the first African American general in the U.S. Army.

Franklin D. Roosevelt is elected in November for an unprecedented third term as president of the United States.

The Selective Service Act becomes law, and some thirty million American men, three million of them black, register for the draft.

1941 A. Philip Randolph announces his March on Washington Movement. The big march is scheduled for July 1.

President Roosevelt meets with Randolph and Walter White at the White House, just two weeks before the Washington march.

On June 25, Roosevelt announces creation of the Fair Employment Practices Commission.

The first black men join the Army Air Corps, July 19.

The Japanese attack Pearl Harbor on Sunday morning, December 7.

The day after the attack on Pearl Harbor, the United States declares war against Japan.

Italy and Germany declare war on the United States, December 11.

1942   The Pittsburgh *Courier* proposes the Double V Campaign.

The 93rd Infantry Division is activated on May 15 at Fort Huachuca, Arizona.

The Marine Corps accepts the first black recruits in its history on June 1.

The 92nd Infantry Division is activated on October 15 at Camp McClellan, Alabama.

1943   Race riots break out during the summer in numerous cities. The worst riots are in Detroit, New York, and Los Angeles.

The USS *Mason*, a destroyer escort, and the PC 1264, a submarine chaser, are the first ships in the navy to have all-black crews. The officers are white.

Italy surrenders on September 8, but the German army controls half of the country.

1944   The army's first company of black paratroopers is the 555th Parachute Infantry Company. Its nickname is the "Triple Nickel." The paratroopers are assigned to fight forest fires in the northwestern United States.

The Women's Naval Corps accepts its first black recruit.

The 93rd arrives in the Solomon Islands.

On June 6, the D-Day invasion begins.

The 370th Infantry Regimental Combat Team, 92nd Infantry Division, arrives in Naples, Italy.

Paris is liberated by the Allies, August 25.

The remainder of the 92nd Infantry Division arrives in Italy in October.

The Germans launch a huge attack in December against the Allies in Belgium, beginning the six-week Battle of the Bulge.

General Dwight D. Eisenhower, on December 26, asks black soldiers to volunteer for frontline combat duty.

1945   Franklin D. Roosevelt dies, April 12. He was president for thirteen years, longer than any other president.

German forces surrender, May 8.

Colonel Benjamin O. Davis Jr. is appointed commander of the all-black 477th Bomb Group at Godman Air Field near Louisville, Kentucky. He is the first African American to command a U.S. military base.

The first atomic bomb is dropped on the Japanese city of Hiroshima, August 6.

The second atomic bomb is dropped on Nagasaki, August 9.

On September 2, the Japanese surrender. World War II is over.

1954   The last racially segregated unit of the armed forces is abolished.

1997   Seven African American World War II veterans receive Medals of Honor in January, at the White House.

Further Reading

Anderson, Jervis. *A. Philip Randolph: A Biographical Portrait* (Berkeley: University of California Press, 1986).

Brandt, Nat. *Harlem at War: The Black Experience in WWII* (Syracuse: Syracuse University Press, 1996).

Davis, Benjamin O. *Benjamin O. Davis Jr., American: An Autobiography* (New York: Plume, 1992).

Francis, Charles E. *The Tuskegee Airmen: The Men Who Changed a Nation* (Boston: Branden Publishing Co., 1997).

Freedman, Russell. *Franklin Delano Roosevelt* (New York: Clarion, 1990).

———. *Eleanor* (New York: Clarion, 1993).

Haskins, James. *The March on Washington* (New York: HarperCollins, 1993).

———. *Black Eagles: African Americans in Aviation* (New York: Scholastic, 1995).

Killens, John Oliver. *And Then We Heard the Thunder* (Washington, D.C.: Howard University Press, 1983).

McGowen, Tom. *Lonely Eagles and Buffalo Soldiers: African Americans in World War II* (New York: Franklin Watts, 1995).

Potter, Lou, with William Miles and Nina Rosenblum. *Liberators: Fighting on Two Fronts in World War II* (New York: Harcourt, Brace & Company, 1992).

Rogasky, Barbara. *Smoke and Ashes: The Story of the Holocaust* (New York: Holiday House, 1988).

Index

Page numbers in *italics* refer to maps and photos.